Lessons for the Urban Witch:

Witchcraft and Magick for Urban Wiccans: Wicca and Magick for Modern Witches

By: Kristina Benson

Lessons for the Urban Witch: Witchcraft and Magick for Urban Wiccans: Wicca and Magick for Modern Witches

ISBN 978-1-60332-000-9

Printed in the United States of America

Table of Contents

INTRODUCTION

Although today's Wicca is a religion and a way of life only fifty or sixty years old, there still are still challenges to practicing and honoring the Wiccan way in a modern, and inevitably urban, environment.

One of the most obvious challenges involves the ability to commune with nature—after all, many Wiccan rituals take place in nature and nearly all worship it. Urban Wiccans will generally have a difficult time finding a forest, rock, or brook to commune with, not to mention a huge problem seeing the moon and stars through the layer of electric lighting and smog that obscures the night sky.

Nature, however, is still in the city. Every weed or flower that wriggles through a crack in the sidewalk, every tree that fragments the concrete surrounding it with its immense root structure, every bird whose song can be heard over the roar of traffic—all of these things are reminders that nature still survives. Finding nature wherever you are and sorting through the urban energy to find the Magic is a challenge, to be sure, but it is not impossible.

With a little effort, the modern Wiccan can connect with the elements without having to move or plan elaborate trips out of the city. This book will give suggestions to the urban Wicca, and share some rituals and practices that can help you tune in with nature wherever you are.

MODERN LIVING LESSONS

FINDING THE ELEMENTS IN THE CITY

As we all know, Wiccan tradition states that there are five elements. It is through these elements and their constituents that all things are created, and made to exist. The elements are Air, Fire, Water, Earth, and Spirit. This assertion is not meant to be taken literally—they merely represent five forces or energies that are present in all things.

These five elements are also represented by the equilateral cross which. This is the keystone of the Wiccan altar and magic circle. Though the order and placement of the elements within this cross can be any way you like, the traditional placement is used here and is based on the four cardinal points of the compass.

The two heavy elements are Earth and Water, and are Passives. The two light elements are Air and Fire, and they are Actives. Earth is the opposite of Air, and Fire is the opposite of Water.

There are also five elements of the human individual, which are similarly not to be taken literally: the mind, the heart, the soul, the body, and the essence.

Finding the elements in the city can be challenging, but not impossible. The biggest challenge of all is Air, as urban environments are often clogged with smoke and smog and soot and all kinds of other impurities.

There are fortunately, however, ways in which you can assure that at least the air in your home is as clean as possible. Plants are both a way to get in touch with the Earth, and a way to clean and purify the air in your home. Having as many plants as possible will clean the air, absorb some of the airborne toxins, and bring nature's energy into the space. Purchasing a small humidifier can also help to make sure the air in your home is to your liking. In dry, desert environments a humidifier can benefit the lungs and the skin, and can assure that tropical types of plants will thrive.

I do not recommend the use of air fresheners, as they are usually just scented chemicals. They may create the illusion of cleanliness, but all they are really doing is adding chemicals to your house. Keeping open containers of baking soda in the house can help absorb bad odors, and burning high-quality incense and chemicals can improve the smell of a home greatly. I find, however, that the best way to make my home smell inviting is to bake frequently, clean out the refrigerator on a regular basis, vacuum constantly, and cultivate as many sweet-smelling flowers as possible.

Water, luckily, is easy to come across with the help of a filter. Purchasing bottled water is always an option but this involves wasting plastic. Plastic comes from petroleum, and is has been suggested that some of the chemicals in the bottles can leak into the water contained within. As a result, I generally prefer to use filtered tap water.

Fire is not a big issue in an urban environment, as one only has to strike a match or light the fireplace. Danger from fire, however, is magnified in an indoor setting. Make sure that you always have a fire extinguisher handy if you are going to be lighting candles or incense, and never ever leave these things unattended. As long as these simple precautions are taken, fire is easy to come by.

Earth can be tough for those who do not have a yard or live in an apartment. Keeping potted plants, however, is an easy solution to this problem. It can often be easier to tend an indoor garden because one doesn't have to keep such a vigilant watch over the plants during times of a cold snap, heat wave, or dry spell.

APARTMENT FRIENDLY RITUALS

Luckily, rituals and spells can be practiced anywhere: outdoors, in a special room or space in a house, in a shared area devoted solely to ritual work and magic. The space you choose can be anywhere in your home as long it is one in which you feel safe and will have at least some privacy. It should ideally be one where roommates or family members will not interfere with your altar or your tools, and will not be likely to interrupt or intrude. Of course, there is no private space in your dwelling, there is nothing wrong with taking out your altar when you need it and putting it away when you're finished with it. It's even ok to practice in your bathroom or closet, if those are the only private spaces you have.

You will want enough room, however, to be able to stand straight up with your arms spread all the way out. You should not feel crowded or cramped, or feel as though you can't move without knocking something over.

The following is a list of rituals that can take place indoors, in a small space.

THE BATH OR SHOWER

Before performing spell work, concocting a potion, or even engaging in deep meditation, it is necessary to take a ritual bath. Though many prefer baths to showers, there are many apartments that don't have bathtubs. In this case, a shower is perfectly acceptable. Those that wish to practice in a coven will be expected to have taken a ritual bath before appearing for initiation and other important ceremonies.

You will need:
A small silver or porcelain bowl with spring water
Sea salt
A white candle
Incense of your choice
Oils or herbs of your choice

Select a time and place where you know that you will be undisturbed. Lock the door and turn off the phone, if need be. Draw a hot bath and add some essence, oils, or herbs. Figure out which herbs will benefit you the most. For example, merely wishing to cleanse and purify, sage might be a good choice. If about to perform a love charm, rose oil might be better.

Turn off all the lights and light a single white taper. The white taper should be unused, and should have a candle holder that will allow you to put it down and not worry about it. A simple votive candle will do if no taper is available.

Light a stick of incense or place some on a glowing coal in a censer that you can pick up, and sprinkle a pinch of sea salt in a white dish or silver bowl. If you are planning to take a shower, a few small modifications will be necessary. Instead of passing the magical tools over the bathwater, as you will be instructed, pass the tools over the space in which you will be showering. Mix the salt, oils, and herbs together to make a scrub to use in the bath.

If you are taking a bath: once the bath is drawn and any oils have been added to it as desired, take the candle and make three slow passes over the water.

> Say: "By this fire I purify this bathwater. May all impurities, contaminants, and evil energies flee before its light."

Set the candle down, making sure it's somewhere where it can flicker freely without worry of setting anything on fire or being knocked over.

Sprinkle the sea salt in the bathwater.

> *Say: "With this I purify this ritual bath. May all impurities, contaminants, and evil energies flee from it."*

Set down the dish and pick up the incense, or, if you wish, bundle of smoldering sage.

> *Say: "By this smoke I purify this ritual bath. May my good energy and aspirations be carried in the smoke to the Lady. "*

Set down the incense. Pour the water into the bath. It can be spring water, rain water, or ocean water.

> *Say: "By this I purify this ritual bath. May this bath contain the Waters of Life that spring from Mother Earth."*

Undress and enter your bath. Enjoy it for as long as you want. Use this time to meditate on that which you wish to accomplish. Dry off with a freshly cleaned towel that has been allowed to line dry outside if at all possible. The color of the towel can be coordinated with the work you intend to do.

Anoint yourself with whatever oils you plan to use. Dress in ritual robes or other clothing if you must drive or walk to the site where you will be working the craft.

There will be times when the full ritual bath is not feasible. You may cleanse and consecrate special water and keep it in a bottle for emergencies.

CANDLES

One of the simplest of magical arts is candle burning. The materials are easy to obtain and use an object with which we are all familiar—a candle. You can do it in any space, shared or unshared, and as you will only need a candle, the magical tools won't be expensive.

The size and shape of the candles you use is unimportant, although decorative, extra large, ornate, scented, or unusually shaped candles will not be suitable as these may create distractions. The simple slender candles sold for use in the home is perfectly fine, if not ideal. Those who are feeling particularly industrious can make his or her own. Candle kits can be found at specialty and craft stores, and are easy to use.

The candles you use for any type of magical use should be completely unused, and no one but yourself should touch it. Under no circumstances use a candle which has already been lit, even for the most benign purpose. Vibrations picked up by secondhand materials or equipment may disturb and pollute your work.

Once you have purchased or made your ritual candle it has to be 'dressed' before burning so as to establish a psychic link between it and you. By touching the candle during the dressing procedure, you are charging it with our own personal energy and also concentrating the desire of your magical act into the wax. The candle, in this sense, almost becomes like a wand, and is an extension of you. Make sure you dress the candle before it is lit.

To dress it, point the candle to the north. Use a compass to make sure that you are pointing it in the right direction. Rub oil into the candle beginning at the top or North end and work downwards to the half-way point. Always brush in the same direction downwards. This process is then repeated by beginning at the bottom or south end and working up to the middle. The oil that you use is important. This will be discussed later in detail.
The candles you use can be colored in accordance with the following magical uses:

White- peace and innocence

Red- strength, courage, sexual potency

Pink- love and romance

Yellow- memory

Green- fertility and luck

Blue-protection from evil

Purple- luck in finances

Orange—career matters

For instance, if you wanted to use candle magic to enrich your sex life, you would select a red candle to burn. To pass an exam, burn a yellow candle.

The simplest form of candle magic is to write down your goal on a clean, unused piece of paper. Use paper in a color that matches the candle. As you write your goal, visualize your dream coming true. Visualize your boss giving you a raise, or your business selling out of its product because it has become a wild success.

After you have written down your goal and meditated on it,

carefully fold the paper four times. Place the end of the folded paper in the candle flame and set light to it.

MAKE SURE YOU HAVE A FIRE EXTINGUISHER HANDY. Or at the very least, have a glass of water around. As it burns, focus on your goal.

Allow the candle to burn till it goes out. Take normal fire safety precautions and keep watch over it as it burns.

If you are conducting a magical ritual which involves another person, such as sending healing powers to a sick person, the second person can be symbolically present during the ritual by another candle.

EASY SPELLS FOR THE URBAN WITCH

SPELL TO MEND A WOUNDED HEART

To Ease a Broken Heart you will need the following
ingredients (be sure to charge them all before you begin):

Strawberry tea (at least one teabag's worth)

Small wand or stick from a willow tree

Three drops of lavender oil.

pink candles (2)

a mirror

one pink drawstring bag

one quartz crystal

one bowl of china, crystal, or silver

one silver spoon

1 teaspoon dried jasmine

1 tsp. strawberry leaves

1 teaspoon cloves

20 drops strawberry oil

Arrange the materials on a small table. Light an unused,
pink candle that has been rubbed in a drop of strawberry

oil. Make sure that no one has touched the candle besides you, and make sure that the candle has never been used. Make strawberry tea and when the water is done boiling, let the tea steep. While it steeps, draw a bath and add the lavender. Do not use any light other than the pink candle's light to draw and take the bath. If you do not have a bathtub, make a salt scrub out of the herbs, oils, and salt to use in the shower.

When you emerge, sip the strawberry tea. Put a dab of strawberry oil on your throat, wrists, and heart. Use the willow wand to cast two circles in a clockwise direction around the table that the materials rest on.
Rub two drops of strawberry oil on the second candle. Make sure that the wick end is pointed north as you do so. Light the second pink candle. Mix all remaining oils and herbs—except for the strawberry tea leaves from the tea--in the bowl.

While you stir the mixture slowly clockwise with a silver spoon, look at yourself in the mirror and say aloud:

"I see the Threefold Goddess within me."

Then put the mixture in the pink bag with the crystal. You will carry it with you always. Every time you are tempted to dwell on that which wounded your heart, smell the bag full of herbs. Remind yourself that you are the Threefold Goddess, and you bask in the light of Diana.

When your heart is healed, bury the bag in the soil of a potted plant, preferably one with a flowering plant.

HOME PROTECTION SPELL

You will need:

>   Small mirror
>   Seven white candles
>   Bundle of dried sage
>   Matches
>   Essential oil of your choosing
>   Representation of the Goddess of your choosing
>   Representation of the God of your choosing

As always, the first step is to consecrate the space you will be using, take a bath or shower, and put on your ritual wear.

Place your God and Goddesses representations in the middle of the altar. The next step will be to dress your candles. Kneel before the altar. Using essential oil from an herb or tree with protective qualities, mentally visualize a wall of energy surrounding your home. Rub the candles with the oil, pointing the wicks North as you do so.

Next, go to your altar. After reaching a state of concentration, place a bundle of sage between the effigies of the Goddess and the God. Ring the sage and effigies with your candles. Turn to your Goddess effigy. Continuing to visualize the field of energy surrounding your home, say:

> *"Lunar light protect me!"*

Then turn to the God and say:

> *"Solar light protect me!"*

Repeat as you light each candle.
Now, holding the mirror, invoke the Goddess and say:

> *"Great Goddess of the Light*
> *Great Goddess of the Sea*
> *Great Goddess of the Land*
> *Let all darkness flee."*

Standing before the altar, hold the mirror facing the candles so that it reflects their flames. Keeping the mirror toward the candles, move slowly clockwise around your altar seven times, repeating the invocation. Continue concentrating on the wall of energy that surrounds your home. Visualize the candle light burning away the bad energy in your home.

Then, invoke the God and say:

> *"Great God of the Light*
> *Great God of the Sea*
> *Great God of the Land*
> *Let all darkness flee."*

As you say this, hold the mirror as you have been but move counter clockwise, repeating the invocations.

Charge your home with the protective light of the Goddess and God. Visualize the light streaming through your home and bathing it in light.

When finished, stand once again before the images. Thank the Goddess and the God in any words you wish. Put out the candles, tie them together with white cord and store them in a safe place.

BASIC PROSPERITY SPELL

This is a basic spell that if used correctly, will bring you money.

You will need:

> 1 gold candle
> 6 green candles
> 9 white candles
> Pine oil
> sea salt or, if you live near the ocean, sand.

Take your ritual bath, put on your ritual wear, and cast the circle. Then carefully dress all candles with pine oil.

Arrange the candles thusly on the altar:

Gold candle in the center
Green candles in a circle around gold candle
White candles in a circle around green candles.

To begin, sprinkle a circle of salt or sand around the altar. Start to concentrate. Visualize yourself walking down the street and finding money, a bank error in which you are given extra funds or even a mound of coupons to your oft-frequented stores.

Light the middle candle and envision the flame acting as a magnet for money.

Circle the altar three times clockwise, visualizing the luck you want.

Say the following three times:

> *"As my heart be full with the Goddess' light*
> *Bring money into my sight."*

After the previous saying, snuff out the flames. Place the candles in a green bag, and put them away. Though they cannot be used for another spell, they can serve decorative purposes at a later date.

SELF BLESSING

This can be performed on the eve of a Sabbat, during a particularly challenging time, or in honor of a new moon.

The purpose of the ritual is to bring you into closer contact with the Goddess and the God, to feel their blessings, and to reaffirm the relationship you have with them. It may also be used to banish any negative influences which may have formed around the person, to cleanse oneself after contact with someone who has contagious negative energy, or on another person who requires any of the above. After the ritual, it is ideal that the blessed person spend time in meditation, or in solitude, reflecting on that which has transpired. It is also ideal that the participants be sky-clad, though this is not necessary.

You will need:
> Sea salt or sand from a beach or riverbank
> Three red or green grapes
> Spring water
> White candle

After taking a ritual bath, cast your circle. Sprinkle the salt on the floor and stand on it. Light your candle and enjoy its warmth. Imagine its light and energy surrounding you and mingling with your own energy. Say:

> *"Bless me, mother, for I am a child of the earth, and the eyes of the world."*

Dip the fingers of the right hand into the water and touch to your eyelids, first the left, then the right. Say:

> *"Blessed be my eyes, that I may see your works and majesty".*

Touch the water to the tip of the nose. Say:

> *"Blessed be my nose, that I may breathe the wind and air."*

Touch the water to the top lip, then the bottom, then the tip of the tongue. Say:

> *"Blessed be my tongue that I may speak of you."*

Touch the water to your chest. Say:

> *"Blessed be my breast, that I may feel your love in my heart."*

Touch your feet, first the left, then the right. Say:

> *"Blessed be my feet that I may walk in your ways."*

Eat the grapes, one after the other, and Say:

> *"Blessed be your bounty that I may enjoy of your gifts."*

Enjoy the candle for as long as you wish. If desired, set it down and meditate. When you exit the circle, try to spend at least an hour in solitude and reflection.

BASIC LOVE SPELL

For this spell, you will need:
- 2 pink candles
- 3 cloves
- 2 teaspoons of black tea
- 3 pinches cinnamon
- 3 pinches nutmeg
- 3 fresh mint leaves
- 6 fresh rose petals
- 6 lemon leaves
- 3 cups pure spring water
- Brown sugar
- Honey

Brew this tea on a Friday during a waxing moon. Take your ritual bath as usual, but with pink candles. As you bathe, focus on the work you are about to do.

Cleanse and consecrate a tea kettle and teapot. Cast your circle, and light a pink candle to place on your altar. Boil the spring water, pour into tea pot, and place the tea pot on your altar. Let the herbs steep. As it is brewing,

Recite this verse three times:

> *"I MAKE THIS TEA BY THE LIGHT OF THE*
> *MOON TO MAKE [lover's name] ONLY FOR ME*
> *SWOON!"*

Pour in the honey and the sugar, and then add to your cup. Drink one sip of the tea and say:

> *"GODDESS OF LOVE, I BREWED THIS TEA*
> *THAT [lover's name] MAY DESIRE ME!"*

On the following Friday, brew another pot of the tea and share it with the object of your affections. He or she will soon begin to fall in love with you.

BASIC SPELL TO ATTRACT LOVE

You Will Need:

> 1 Pink Candle
> Rose Incense
> Rosemary leaves
> 4 Drops Tangerine oil

First, dress your candle in Tangerine oil, and take ritual bath by its light. When you emerge, take the candle with you, sit before your altar and concentrate. Think of the qualities you have to give to another, and the qualities you want him/her to be able to give to you.

As you concentrate, sprinkle the rosemary around the candle.

Say:

> *"I say to the spirits of the Lady above,*
> *I am ready to meet my one true love."*

Say this as many times as needed, and as you do so, imagine a vivid pink light emanating from your body and filling the room. When you are finished, extinguish the flame.

CROSSING PATHS SPELL

You Will Need:

> Yellow candles
> Yellow thread
> Picture of yourself
> Picture of intended
> Magnet or moonstone
> Scissors
> Yellow thread
> Yling Ylang oil

On a night during the Waxing Moon, gather the above ingredients, dress your candles with the yling ylang oil, and take your ritual bath by their light.

When you emerge, bring the candles. Hold your picture in your left hand, and hold the other picture in your right.

Say:

> *"I hold your picture in my hand*
> *By the will of the Lady*

You will soon before me stand."

As you say this, cut the images out of the photos, and then sew them together with the needle and thread. Place the picture underneath the moonstone or magnet on your altar, between two of the yellow candles.

Say:

> *"This picture of me,*
> *This picture of you*
> *Now are one when*
> *Once they were two."*

Meditate as long as you need. Though the spell has been cast, you must still continue to send energy to the person you want to see, as well as contact him or her.

FIDELITY SPELL

This very simple, very easy spell acts to strengthen the bonds that keep lovers faithful.

You Will Need:

> 1 lime
> Hair From Your Head
> Hair From Your Partners Head
> Pink candle
> Ritual bowl

This spell should ideally be done on a Friday when the moon is waxing. Take your bath by the light of the pink candle. When you emerge, go to your altar. Place the hairs in the ritual bowl and squeeze the lime juice on them, saying:

> *"I am bound to you*
> *You are bound to me*
> *By the light of the moon*
> *So mote it be."*

Repeat this as many times as necessary.

CINNAMON SPELL

This spell will add spice to your love life.

You Will Need:

>3 Tablespoons Of Cinnamon Powder
>A red piece of fabric
>A length of red lace
>Red candle
>Yling Ylang oil
>Rose quartz

The Spell:

Dress your candle in the oil and take your ritual bath by its light. When you emerge, cast your circle, and place the cinnamon powder and rose quartz in the fabric. Holding the fabric in your right hand, say,

>*"Spicing up my love life,*
>*the Goddess in my heart,*
>*Bring me the frenzy this spell will start."*

Carry the handkerchief in your bag for at least a week.

HERBALISM FOR THE URBAN WICCAN

Many herbal medicine books, and books about Wicca, refer to picking wild herbs or cultivating them in a garden. As a city dweller, I haven't had a house with a garden since I moved out of my parents' house in the suburbs, and I doubt that I am alone in this. An additional concern for the Urban Wiccan is one of cost. Though health food stores and herbal stores are easy to find, their wares are more often than not extremely pricey. The following is a list of herbs and herbal remedies that are easy to find in most any grocery store, and by and large, are fairly affordable.

APPLE
Malus domestica

HISTORY AND USES
Apples are one of the most widely cultivated and consumed fruits. Research suggests that the consumption of apples may reduce the risk of colon cancer, prostate cancer and lung cancer. Apples also contain a naturally occurring antioxidant that has shown some promise in protecting cells from the effects of stress

Apple consumption can help remove food stuck between the teeth, but the acid contained in the fruit is also capable of eroding tooth enamel over time, so eating an apple should not be a substitute for tooth brushing. Raw, overripe, or baked apple can be made into a poultice to treat a sprain, or put over the eyes to relieve eyestrain. Apple water can also reduce a fever.

APRICOT/APRICOT SEED
Prunus armeniaca

HISTORY AND USES

The apricot fruit comes from a tree that is thought to have originated in China, and was brought to Europe by the Moors when they invaded and took over Spain.

Laetrile, which has long been considered a treatment for cancer, is extracted from apricot seeds. As early as the year 502, apricot seeds were used to treat tumors and ulcers. The American Medical Association, however, does not substantiate the effectiveness of laetrile.

Apricots have also been used as an aphrodisiac, and to stimulate uterine contractions.

ARROWROOT
Maranta arundinacea (Marantaceae)

HISTORY and USES

Arrowroot is native to South America and the Caribbean. The indigenous peoples in these areas have long used its root as a poultice for sores, and as an infusion to treat urinary tract infections. It can also be used as a soothing agent on inflamed mucous membrane tissue, a nutrient in convalescence, and for easing digestion. It helps to relieve acidity, indigestion and colic, and can act as a gentle laxative. It may be applied as an ointment, demulcent, or poultice mixed with some other antiseptic herbs such as comfrey.

BEET
beta vulgaris

HISTORY AND USES

Though the root is used for cooking in the west, it is possible to use the tops of the beet as salad greens. The root is extremely versatile, and can be peeled, steamed or baked, and then eaten warm with butter; or peeled, shredded raw, and then eaten as a salad. The Romans used beet root as a treatment for fevers and constipation, to bind wounds, and as an aphrodisiac.

CABBAGE

HISTORY AND USES

Cabbages are flowering plants of the family Brassicaceae, and are related to the wild mustard plant. In European folk medicine, cabbage leaves are used to treat acute inflammation. One leaf can be dipped in water and placed on a wound in order to alleviate discomfort. It should be replaced after it gets warm from the wound. It also can help infected wounds and draw out pus in the same manner. One of the chemicals in cabbage can also treat respiratory papillomavirus.

CAYENNE PEPPER
Capsicum Solanaceae

HISTORY AND USES

Cayenne, consumed in powdered form, or as raw fruit, has been used as medicine for centuries. It is the most effective blood stimulant ever studied. In addition, it has endorphin-stimulating properties. It can treat stomachaches, cramping pains, and gas. If rubbed on the skin, it can act as an irritant, which, oddly enough, can be beneficial if rubbed on an area of the skin that has already been irritated. It can also be gargled as a wash to improve a sore throat. Some studies suggest that it can act as an appetite suppressant, and can help even out spikes in blood sugar.Cayenne peppers are high in Vitamin C, Vitamin B, potassium, and iron.

CELERY
Apium graveolens (Umbelliferae)

HISTORY and USES

Although celery is now very common in culinary pursuits, it also has many fine healing properties. It's mainly used in the treatment of rheumatism, arthritis and gout. The seeds are also used as a urinary antiseptic. It is a very good cleansing herb, and a powerful diuretic, and can help in expelling waste and toxins. The seeds also have a reputation as a carminative with a mild tranquilizing effect. The stems are less significant medicinally, but are certainly useful in the kitchen.

CINNAMON

Cinnamomum verum syn. C. zeylanicum (Lauraceae)

HISTORY and USES

Cinnamon is native to Sri Lanka, and grows best in tropical forest climates. Cinnamon has long been used in India and Egypt for medicinal purposes. To this day, it is, of course, a common spice in cooking, and is used in perfumery. The infusion or powder is excellent to help alleviate stomach pains and cramps. There is also some evidence that cinnamon can help smooth out spikes in blood sugar. Cinnamon is also useful as a household insecticide and to keep away ants—if sprinkled on a trail of ants, the ants will die, and will be less likely to return. Traditionally, the herb was taken for colds, flu and digestive problems.

CUMIN
Nigella sativa

HISTORY AND USES

Cumin seeds have a bitter flavor and smell a bit like strawberries. It is a common household herb for cooking and flavoring liquor. Ibn Sina, known to westerners as Avicenna, refers to black cumin as a seed that stimulates the body's energy and helps recovery from fatigue and dispiritedness. He also describes it as having a positive effect on treating digestive disorders, gynecological diseases and respiratory ailments.

The seeds have been used in the Middle East and Southeast Asian countries to treat Asthma, Bronchitis, Rheumatism and related inflammatory diseases, to increase lactation, in nursing mothers, to promote digestion, and to fight parasitic infections. Its oil has been used to treat skin conditions such as eczema and boils.

GARLIC
Allium sativum (Liliaceae)

HISTORY AND USES

Garlic is originally from central Asia but was used as flavoring and medication by the Egyptians, Greeks, and Romans. Garlic is still incredibly useful. It is one of the most effective anti-biotic plants commonly available, acting on bacteria, viruses and alimentary parasites. The cloves can counter nose, throat and chest, and can act as an expectorant. It will also act as a palliative for congested sinuses and can help clear blocked nasal passages to bring relief in cases of bad allergies or a cold. Garlic is also known to reduce cholesterol, increase circulation, lower blood pressure, and lower blood sugar levels. It can also help to expunge parasites, such as worms, from the body.

HONEY

HISTORY AND USES

For at least 2700 years, honey has been used to treat a variety of ailments through topical application. Antibacterial properties of honey are the result of a hydrogen peroxide like behavior on a chemical level, and high acidity. Topical honey has been used successfully in a comprehensive treatment of diabetic ulcers and antioxidants in honey have been shown to reduce the damage done to the colon in colitis. Furthermore, some studies suggest that honey may be effective in increasing the populations of good bacteria in the digestive tract, which may help strengthen the immune system, improve digestion, lower cholesterol, and prevent cancer of the colon.

Some studies suggest that the topical use of honey may reduce odors, swelling, and scarring when used to treat wounds; it may also prevent the dressing from sticking to a wound that is healing.

LEMON
Citrus Limon (Rutaceae)

HISTORY AND USES

A native from Asia, it was first introduced to Europe by the Arabs when they were in control of Spain. It is now widely cultivated in Italy, California and Australia. It is an important and versatile natural medicine. It is cheap, readily available, and can easily be used at home. Lemons have a high vitamin C content that helps improve resistance to infection, and can reduce the duration of a cold or flu. It is taken as a preventative for stomach infections, circulatory problems and arteriosclerosis. Lemon juice and oil are effective in killing germs. Lemon juice also decreases inflammation and improves digestion. Drinking a cup of lemon tea can help soothe a fever, and eating a lemon slice can help relieve sinus congestion.

NUTMEG
Myristica fragrans/argentea/otoba

HISTORY AND USES

The essential oil taken from steaming ground nutmeg is currently used often in cosmetics and perfumery. There is anecdotal evidence that nutmeg and nutmeg oil can treat problems of the nervous and digestive systems.

Externally, the oil can be topically applied to provide relief from rheumatic pain and can be applied to an infected or decayed tooth to quell the pain. Using a few drops of nutmeg oil on a sugar lump, a small piece of fruit, or in a teaspoon of honey or maple syrup can act as a cure for nausea, gastroenteritis, chronic diarrhea, and indigestion.

A massage oil to treat muscle pain and ache can be made by mixing 10 drops of nutmeg in 10 ml almond oil.

OATMEAL

HISTORY AND USES

"Oatmeal" is used to describe any crushed or rolled oats from a variety of species of plants. It is an excellent, gentle food to eat when convalescing or ill. It can also be made into a paste to ease itching, hives, or insect bites. Dissolving it in the bath will soothe sunburned skin.

ONION
Allium cepa

HISTORY AND USES

This popular household food is native to Central Asia, and evidence suggests that onions may be effective in treating the common cold, heart disease, and diabetes. They can act as anti-inflammatory, and have anti-cholesterol, anticancer, and antioxidant components.
In homeopathy, onion is used for rhinorrhea and hay fever.

Onions are very rich in chromium, a mineral that helps cells respond to insulin, plus vitamin C, and numerous flavonoids.

The higher the intake of onion, the lower the level of glucose found during oral or intravenous glucose tolerance tests. This means that onions could possibly be helpful in controlling spikes in blood sugar.

The regular consumption of onions has, like garlic, been shown to lower high cholesterol levels and high blood pressure, and to be a very effective anti-inflammatory and expectorant. In addition quercetin, and other flavonoids found in onions, work with vitamin C to help kill harmful bacteria.

OREGANO
Oreganum vulgare

HISTORY AND USES

Oregano is high in antioxidant activity, and has demonstrated antimicrobial activity against food-borne pathogens. In the Philippines, oregano is not commonly used for cooking but is rather considered as a primarily medicinal plant, useful for relieving children's coughs.

THYME
Thymus L

HISTORY AND USES
There are about 350 plants that fit into the genus
"thymus". It was widely used for embalming in ancient
Egypt, and was used by the ancient Greeks to freshen and
purify rooms. Currently, it is primarily known as a useful
culinary herb, though it does have some medicinal
properties.

The essential oil of common thyme is an antiseptic, and is
antifungal.

A tea made by infusing the herb in water can be used for to
treat coughs, irritations of the respiratory tract, and
bronchitis. Because it is antiseptic, thyme boiled in water
and cooled can be gargled to soothe a sore throat. Thyme
tea can cause uterine contractions, and as such, should not
be taken by pregnant women.

WHITE VINEGAR

HISTORY AND USES

Vinegar can be used as an herbicide if diluted to 20% vinegar and 80% water. It may kill some top-growth if a plant is particularly delicate, but will not kill the roots. Vinegar along with hydrogen peroxide is used in the livestock industry to kill bacteria and viruses before refrigeration storage. Hippocrates prescribed vinegar for many ailments, from skin rash to ear infection. Multiple trials indicate that taking vinegar with food increases satiety dramatically, and even a single application of vinegar can lead to reduced food intake for a whole day. Small amounts of vinegar—i.e. two tablespoons per serving--added to food, or taken along with a meal, have been shown by to reduce the glycemic index of carbohydrate food for people with and without diabetes.

Herbal Recipes

CHAKRA OPENING BREW

3 parts Rose petals

1 part Cinnamon

1/2 part Nutmeg

½ part clove

½ part black tea

Place in teapot, fill with boiling water, let steep, covered, for a few minutes. Let it steep and then drink with honey, if desired.

APHRODITE LUST DRINK

2 tsp. Black Tea

1 pinch Coriander

3 fresh Mint leaves (or 1/2 tsp. dried)

5 fresh Rosebud petals (or 1 tsp. dried)

½ tsp dried lemon peel

1 pinch Nutmeg

3 pieces Orange peel

Place all ingredients into teapot. Boil three cups or so of water and add to the pot. Sweeten with honey or maple syrup.

VENUS LUST DRINK

5 parts Rose petals
1/2 part Clove
1/2 part Nutmeg
1 part ginger
1 tsp honey (to taste)

Make as a normal tea

GINGER MINT TEA

Useful for: fever

2g crushed ginger
2g crushed mint leaves
1 ½ c. hot water

Directions: Mix the 2 herbs in the water and bring to a boil. Cover and cook for 15 minutes. Strain the decoction and drink.

ROSEMARY TEA
Useful for: general aches and pains, lack of energy

Directions: boil water, and add one teaspoon of crushed or dried rosemary. Pour through a strainer and serve. Honey may be used as a sweetener

GINGER TEA
Useful for: asthma, respiratory problems

Directions: add ¼ teaspoon of ginger to ½ cup of hot water. Take two tablespoons before bedtime.

HOLY BASIL TEA

Useful for: chronic bronchitis; chronic irritation of the upper respiratory tract

1 tablespoon of basil

2 cups of hot water

Directions: Take two tablespoons four times per day

CINNAMON TEA

Useful for: congestion, common cold

3 g. bark

1 ½ cups of hot water

Directions: Steep and drink at bedtime as tea

CAYENNE PEPPER SHOT

Useful for: extreme congestion, sinus infection

1 cup hot water

1 tsp lemon juice

1 garlic clove put through a garlic press

1 pinch cayenne pepper

Directions: Mix well and take as a shot

FENNEL LINSEED TEA

Useful for: constipation

1/3 tea spoon Fennel seeds, powdered

1/3 tea spoon Linseed seeds, powdered

1/3 tea spoon Liquorice root, powdered

1 3/4 cups Water

Combine equal quantities of the three herbs and add this herb mixture to the water and boil, covered, for 10 minutes. Filter the tea before drinking.

Dosage: 1 cup, 3 times a day.

BLACK PEPPER TEA

Useful for: diarrhea

5 crushed pepper seeds
1 c. water

Directions: Boil the seeds in the water for 15 minutes in a covered container. Remove from the heat and strain. Take 1/2 tea spoon, twice a day.

LEMON TEA

Useful for: cold, fever

1 lemon slice
1 cup hot water

Directions: bring water to a boil. Pour a cup and add the lemon slice. Sip slowly.

YARROW TEA
Useful for: piles

1-2 tea spoon Herb/blossoms, crushed
1 cup Water

Directions: prepare the infusion by combining the herb with the water in a covered container. Let the mixture stand for 5-6 hours. Strain before drinking.

CORIANDER INFUSION
Useful for: impotence

1 tea spoon Leaves, chopped
1 cup Boiling water

To make the infusion, cover the leaves with boiling water. Close the lid of the teapot and leave for 15 minutes, then strain.

Dosage: 2-4 table spoon a day.

Remember: coriander leaf extract acts as an aphrodisiac, while Coriander seed extract suppresses the sex drive.

MINT TEA
Useful for: stomach pain

1 tea spoon spearmint leaves, crushed
2 cups Water

Combine the spearmint leaves and the water and raise the mixture to a boil in a covered container. Remove from the heat and let the tea stand for 15 minutes. Strain before drinking.

Dosage: 1-2 cups a day.

GINGER INFUSION
Useful for: painful menstruation

6 g Embelia, whole plant, powdered
6 g Ginger, dried, powdered
1 3/4 cups Water
6 g Sugar

Mix the two herbs and boil. Remove from the heat, strain and sweeten with the sugar.

Dosage: 3/4 cup a day.

ONION COLD RELIEF

Useful for: extreme congestion; chest colds

1 onion, sliced

Merely keep the sliced onion by the bed of a person who is suffering from horrific chest congestion. A personal testimonial: I once was so sick that I couldn't sleep unless I was sitting up. Otherwise I would be overcome with wracking coughs. I tried everything: codeine, robitussin, liquor, lemon juice, a cayenne pepper shot, a chest rub...nothing worked. I could not sleep. Finally I received a suggestion to slice an onion and leave it by my bed. My room smelled for three days, but I was finally able to sleep peacefully.

NATURAL FLU RELIEF
Useful for: relief from the flu

2 teaspoons cayenne pepper

1 ½ teaspoons salt

1 cup hot chamomile tea

1 cup apple cider vinegar

juice from 1 lemon slice

Combine the cayenne pepper, salt and wet ingredients. Let it seep for about 3 minutes. Drink while hot.

Dosage: 1 -2 cups a day

LIST OF HERBS CATEGORIZED BY AILMENTS

To further help you in your pursuit of frugal kitchen witchery and holistic medicine, here is a list of common ailments, and which types of commonly found herbs and ingredients can help soothe them.

ABUNDANCE: wheat, rye, barley

ACHIEVEMENT: rose, ginger, jasmine

ADDICTION-BREAK: fresh cut grass, cayenne pepper, alfalfa

ADDICTIONS-CURB: anise

AFFECTION-BONDS OF: carnation, marigold

AFTERLIFE, TO INSURE HAPPINESS IN: marjoram, neroli

ALL-WISE: goldenrod, ginkgo biloba

ANCESTORS-HONOR: cypress, laurel, bay

ANGER: alyssum, st. John's Wort to moderate

ANOINTING: acacia, almond, amber, apricot kernel, angelica, carnation, frankincense, high john jasmine, lavender, lily of the valley, lotus, myrrh, rose, rosemary, sage, vervain, wood aloe

APHRODISIAC: ambergris, apricot, basil, beet, cardinal flower, cinnamon, cubeb, dong quai, ginseng, lemon, musk, patchouli, vanilla beans, violet

ATONEMENT: plantain, orange, laurel

ATTRACTION: jasmine, musk, rose, vanilla,

AWAKEN: cayenne, ginger, ginseng, peppercorns

BALANCE: chamomile, jasmine, orange, rose, valerian

BANISH NEGATIVE/UNWANTED SPIRITS: cinnamon, copal

BEAUTY: avocado, belladonna, catnip, clover, cocoa, coffee, flax, ginseng, lavender, maidenhair, rose, yerba santa,

BEWITCHMENT-GUARD AGAINST: nutmeg, wormwood

BLACK ARTS: belladonna, deadly nightshade, hellebore, hemlock, henbane, skullcap

BLESSING, HOUSE: rose, sage

BOLDNESS: basil, pepper, thyme

CALMING: chamomile, jasmine, juniper, lilac, valerian, violet

CAT MAGICK: catnip

CELIBACY, PROMOTE: camphor, chamomile, jasmine, lilac

CENTERING: clary sage

CHAKRAS-OPEN: patchouli, sandalwood

CHASTITY: camphor, chaste tree, coconut, cucumber, hawthorn, job's tears, lavender, pennyroyal, pineapple, sweetpea, vervain, wild lettuce, witch hazel

CLAIRVOYANCE: acacia, anise, bay, broom, dittany of crete, eyebright, hazel, honeysuckle, lettuce, lilac, marigold, moonwort, mugwort, nutmeg, rose, rowan, thyme, wormwood, yarrow

CLEANSING: alkanet, anise, asafetida avens, basil, bay, benzoin, birch, bloodroot, burdock, calamus, camphor, cedar, chamomile, cinnamon, citronella, clove, coconut, dragon's blood, elder, eucalyptus, euphorbia, fennel, feverfew, frankincense, heather, horseradish, hyssop, iris, juniper, lavender, lemon, lemon verbena, lemongrass, life everlasting, lime, lovage, marjoram, mimosa, mullein, musk, myrrh, neroli, oak, orange, parsley, peppermint, pepper tree, pine, plantain, rosemary, rue, saffron, sage, sagebrush, salt, sandalwood, shallot, solomon's seal, thistle/holy, thyme, tobacco, turmeric, valerian, vervain, wood betony, woodruff, yucca

COLDS, WARD OFF: garlic, pepper, ginger

COMFORT: amber, chamomile, cypress, jasmine, rose

COMPASSION: apple, bergamot, orange

CONCENTRATION: ginkgo biloba, lemongrass

CONFIDENCE: jasmine

CONFLICT, PREPARATION FOR: broom, ginger, ginseng,

CONFUSION-RELIEVE: high john

CONSCIOUS MIND: lavender

CONSCIOUSNESS-AWAKEN HIGHER: frankincense, vanilla

CONTROL: bayberry, honeysuckle-remove

COSMIC FORCE: yarrow

COURAGE: allspice, borage, clove, cohosh-black, columbine, dragon's blood, frankincense, mandrake, mullein, musk, nettle, ragweed, rose geranium, tea

DETERMINATION: allspice, dong quai, dragon's blood,

DEFENSE: angelica, basil, bay, bayberry, birch, broom, burdock, cinnamon-confers, cinquefoil, club moss, cypress, dill, dragon's blood, fern, feverfew, fir, frankincense, hawthorn, hazel, heather, holly, jasmine, juniper, marjoram, mistletoe(amulet), mugwort, mullein, oak, patchouli, pepper, pine, rosemary, rowan, rue, St. John's wort, thistle, vervain, wormwood, yarrow

DEMONS: AVERT/WARD OFF: mullein, yarrow

DESPAIR- EXPEL: betony

DESPAIR-OVERCOME: couchgrass
DETERMINATION, COURAGE: allspice, dragon's blood, mullein, musk, rosemary

DEVOTION: honeysuckle, jasmine, lavender, rose, rosemary

DIVINATION: acacia, almond, anise, ash, bay, bistort, broom, camphor, chicory, cinnamon, cherry, citron, clove, corn, corn flowers, dandelion, datura, dodder, eyebright, fig, galangal, goldenrod, ground ivy, hazel, hibiscus, honeysuckle, horse chestnut, st. johns wort, juniper, kava-kava, lemon grass, lettuce, mace, marigold, mastic, meadow rue, meadowsweet, mugwort, mullein, nutmeg, olioliuqui, orange, orris, pansy, patchouli, peppermint, pomegranate, roots, rose-red, rosemary, sandalwood, san pedro, star anise, thyme, wild cherry bark, wild lettuce, willow bark, witch hazel, wormwood, yarrow

DRAGON ENERGY: hyssop, snapdragon

DREAMS: chamomile, lavender, poppy,

DOWSING RODS: witch hazel

DURATION: dandelion

EARTHLY DESIRES: .apple, beet, ginger, rose

ELOQUENCE: aspen

ELVES-MISCHIEVOUS PROTECT FROM: mugwort

EMOTIONS-WARM: nettle

EMOTIONAL PAIN- OVERCOME: blueberry, dandelion, raspberry,

EMPOWERMENT: cocoa, coffee, ephedra, ginger,

ENCHANTMENT: basil, bluebell

ENDURANCE: cayenne, oak, ginseng

ENLIGHTENMENT: amber, sandalwood

ENERGY: allspice, bay, cinnamon, cocoa, coffee, dong quai, dragon's blood, ephedra frankincense, ginseng, grapefruit, holly, lotus, musk, oak, peppermint, rosemary, yarrow

EUPHORIA: bergamot, cinnamon, nutmeg, ylang-ylang

EYE WARD AGAINST: ash

EXORCISM: angelica, arbutus, asafetida, avens, basil, bean, birch, boneset, broom, buckthorn, cedar, clove, clover, copal, cumin, devils bit, frankincense, fumitory, garlic, galangal, heliotrope, horehound, horseradish, job's tears, st johns wort, juniper, lavender, leek, lilac, mallow, mistletoe, mullein, myrrh, nettle, onion, peach, peony, pepper, pepper-cayenne, peppermint, rosemary, rue, sagebrush, snapdragon, sloe, solomon's seal, thistle, tamarisk, turmeric, vervain, vetivert, violet, witch grass, wormwood, yarrow

EYESIGHT: beet, carrot, cornflower

FERTILITY: acorn, agaric, banana, basil, bistort, bodhi, caraway seed, carrot, catnip, chickweed, corn flowers, cuckoo-flower, cucumber, cyclamen, daffodil, dock, fig, geranium, grape, hawthorn, hazel, horsetail, lemon balm-increases, mandrake, mistletoe, mullein, mustard, myrtle, nuts, oak, olive, orange palm-date, patchouli, peach, pine nuts, pomegranate, rose, rosemary, rice, spikenard, sunflower, sweet violet, walnut, wheat

FIDELITY: chili pepper, clover, ivy, coriander, licorice, nutmeg, rhubarb, rye, skullcap, yerba mate

FIERCENESS: cayenne, coffee, cinnamon, ephedra, ginseng, dong quai

FIND LOST OBJECTS: neroli

FIVE-FOLD STAR OF REBIRTH: apples

FOCUS: coffee, ginkgo biloba, lavender

FORTUNE-GOOD: see "luck, good fortune"

GAMBLING LUCK: rose, gardenia

GARDEN MAGICK: apple blossom, cinnamon grape
GHOSTS:BANISH: musk, patchouli, sage

GOOD SPIRITS ONLY ENTER: allspice, irish moss,

GRACE-OBTAIN: periwinkle, violet

GRIEF-RELIEF: aloe

GROUNDING: almond, cedar, hazelnut, pine, patchouli, sandalwood

GROWTH: clover, red clover, patchouli

GUARD: pennyroyal

HAPPINESS: apple blossom, basil, bayberry, catnip, cedar, cinnamon, cocoa, cypress, fir, geranium-rose, hawthorn berry, high john-chase away the blues, hyacinth, jasmine, St. John's wort lavender, lemon, lilac, lily of the valley, loosestrife-purple, pomegranite lotus, marjoram, meadowsweet, neroli, orange, patchouli, purslane, rose, rosemary, saffron, sesame, strawberry, thyme, valerian

HARVEST: acorn, apple, blackberry, blueberry

HEART: lemon balm-

IMPOTENCY-TREAT: cinnamon, beets, blueberries, honey

INCREASE: cowslip, ginger

INFERTILITY: walnut

INTUITION-STRENGTHEN: yarrow

JEALOUSY: garlic

KUNDALINI ENERGY: sandalwood

LONGEVITY: alfalfa, cypress, lavender, linden, lemon, lemon balm,life everlasting, maple, oak, orange, parsley, peach, raspberry leaves, rosemary, sage, tansy, wheat grass

LOVE, GENERAL: aloe, apple blossom, apricot, avocado, avens, beet, birch, bloodroot, brazil nut, chamomile, cherry, cherry wood, chestnut, chickweed, clove, clover, cohosh-black, coltsfoot, columbine, copal, coriander, crocus, cubeb, cumin, daffodil, damiana, devils bit, dill, dogbane, elecampane, elm, endive, eryngo, fern, fig, frankincense, frangipani,, gardenia, gentian, ginseng, goldenrod, grains of paradise, heather, hemp, hibiscus, honeysuckle, house leek, hyacinth, indian paint brush, joe pye weed, lady's mantle, lemon verbena, lettuce, licorice, little john, lime, liverwort, magnolia, male fern, mallow, mandrake, maple, marjoram, mastic, mimosa, mint, moonwort, neroli, nuts, oak moss, ommak, orange, orchid, papaya, patchouli, pea, pear, peach, peppermint, periwinkle, pimento, pistachio, prickly ash, plumaria, primrose, purslane, quince, quassia, raspberry, rowan berry, rue, saffron, san pedro, sarsaparilla, savory, senna, snakeroot, southern wood, spearmint, spiderwort, spikenard, stephanotis, strawberry, sugar cane, sumbul, tamarind, tansy, thyme, tormentil, vervain, violet leaf, wheat, wild cherry bark, wild lettuce, wild rose, willow bark, witch grass, wood aloes, yerba mate, yohimbe

LOYALTY: primrose, rosemary

LUCK/FORTUNE-GOOD: alfalfa, aloe, apple, ash, bamboo, banyon, basil, bayberry, be-still, bluebell, cabbage, calamus, caper, cascara sagrada, catnip, cedar, chamomile, china berry, cinchona, cinnamon, cinquefoil, corn flowers, cubeb, cuckoo-flower, corn, cotton, daisy, daffodil, dandelion, dill, devils shoestring, dragon's blood, eryngo, fern, frankincense, galangal, grains of paradise, hazel, heal all, heather, holly, house leek, huckleberry, honeysuckle, ivy, jasmine, kava-kava, linden, lotus, male fern, mint, moss, nuts, oak, orange persimmon, pineapple, pomegranate, poppy seed, purslane, rose, snakeroot, rue, straw, sumbul, spikenard, star anise, strawberry, tonka

beans, vetivert, vervain, violet, wood aloe, wood rose,
yellow dock

LUST: ambergris, avocado, bergamot, caraway cardamom,
carrot, cattail, celery, cinnamon, civet, clove, clover (red),
cumin, cyclamen, daisy, damiana, deerstongue, devils bit,
dill, dulse, endive, eryngo, garlic, galangal, ginger, ginseng,
grains of paradise, hibiscus, honey, lemongrass, licorice,
magnolia, maguey, mastic, mint, nettle(inducing),
patchouli, pear, peppermint, periwinkle, radish, rosemary,
saffron, sesame, snakeroot-black, southern wood,
stephanotis, sugar cane, tuberose, vanilla, vetch, violet
leaf,, witch grass, yerba mate, yohimbe

MAGICKAL POISON: belladonna, hellebore, hemlock,
henbane

MAGICKAL SPACE-PURIFY: frankincense, sage

MALE SEXUALITY: acorn, yohimbe

MARRIAGE: ivy, mistletoe, neroli, yarrow

MEDITATION: acacia, angelica, anise seeds, bay, bodhi,
chamomile, eucalyptus, gotu kola, hemp, jasmine,

lavender, lotus, magnolia, myrrh, nutmeg, wisteria AID: elecampane DEEP: nag champa, DEEPEN: myrrh

MENTAL ABILITIES: ginkgo biloba, spearmint

MONEY: alfalfa, almond, bayberry, blackberry, bergamot mint, blue flag, bladderwrack, broom, bromeliad, bryony, buckwheat, calamus, cascara sagrada, cashew, cinquefoil, clove, clover, comfrey, corn, dill, dock, elder, fenugreek, flax, fumitory, galangal, goldenrod, golden seal, grains of paradise, grape, heal all, heliotrope, honesty, honeysuckle, hyssop, lucky hand root, mace, mandrake, maple, marjoram, may apple, moonwort, moss, myrtle, nutmeg, oak, oats, onion, orange, pea, pecan, peppermint, periwinkle, pine, pineapple, pipsissewa, poplar, rattlesnake root, rice, sage, sarsaparilla, sassafras, sesame, snakeroot, snakeroot/black, squill, trillium, vervain, vetivert, wheat

MOON BLESSINGS: almond, cherry, willow

NATURE SPELLS: magnolia

NEGATIVITY: BANISH: cinquefoil, clove, patchouli, sage

POWER: bistort

PROJECTION: belladonna, cinnamon, dittany, mugwort

PROTECTION: anise, datura foxglove, lettuce, nutmeg, sage

RIGHT THINKING: buddhist temple blend

RITUAL: ADD ENERGY: carnation

RUNE MAGICK: bracken

SAMHAIN: dandelion

SCRYING: fennel, mugwort

SKILLS: angelica, anise, bay, borage, cinnamon, fennel, mugwort

STRENGTH: ginger, ginseng, lemongrass

SEX: beets patchouli, sandalwood, yohimbe, ylang-ylang

SPIRITS: angelica, nutmeg, wormwood

THIEVES PROTECT FROM: agave prickly pear cactus, thistle

TOOLS-CONSECRATE: cypress, rose, sage .

TRIPLE GODDESS: rue, trefoil-clover, wild pansy, wood avens

TRIUMPH: laurel, oak leaves

VAMPIRES-REPEL: garlic

VIRILITY, INCREASE:

WINTER INCENSE: pine

WOMAN'S LOVE-ATTRACT: henbane, musk, rose

KITCHEN WITCHERY AND TINCTURES

Tinctures can be found in most herbal, Wiccan, and natural stores. They are, however, expensive. Why not make your own? Again, there are plenty of options for foodstuffs, herbs, and spices commonly found in your cupboard.

Tincture Magic

Tinctures are used for anointment and aromatherapy, and should not be ingested! Furthermore, use with caution until you make sure that you aren't allergic to any of the ingredients in a tincture. People with sensitive skill should be particularly cautious.

Oils are widely used in magic to stimulate consciousness through the olfactories, and tinctures are just as effective. In magical perfumery, a tincture is created by soaking dried plant materials in alcohol. It is very easy to do, and much cheaper than purchasing tinctures on line or at herbal medicine type stores. Plus, you can make your own tinctures and refine your own recipes.

Making Tinctures

For tincturing you need an alcohol of at least 70 percent strength, or 140 proof. Vodka, unfortunately, isn't strong enough.

You will also need dried herbs, fruits, or plants. The not-dried ones won't work! To dry a plant hang it upside down in the sun, or just lay it in the windowsill where it can get the sun's rays. If the climate is too humid or the sun too weak, the herbs may just rot. So experiment with where you place the herbs and at what time of day.

Next, empower and consecrate the herb, and then pour into a small, amber or dark bottle with a tight-fitting lid. Using a small funnel, pour just enough ethyl alcohol into the bottle to wet and cover the herb. Cap tightly. Shake the bottle vigorously every day for a week or two.

Then, using a coffee filter, strain the alcohol. If it's not strong enough, add more herbs and enough alcohol to cover them.

To correctly determine whether the tincture is properly scented, apply a drop or two to your wrist. Wait until the alcohol has evaporated and then smell your wrist. Remember, each scent smells differently on people because it combines with their pheromones in different ways. That's why it's important to try perfumes before you buy them, and let them sit on your skin for at least an hour to see how they mix with your natural scent. Even if one doesn't mix well with your scent, however, you can use it on sachets, pillows, or other household objects, or for anointing magical objects.

After you have tested the smell of your tincture and you are satisfied, filter it one last time through the coffee filter, and add a few drops of castor oil or glycerin. Store in an amber bottle in a cool place for future use.

Easy Tinctures

Guardian Tincture

Cinnamon
Cedar
Clove

Anoint yourself or objects for protection.

Mind Clearing Tincture

Sage
Thyme
Rosemary

Anoint your body and healing amulets with this tincture.

Love Tincture

Orange peel
Rose Petals
Vanilla bean

Cinnamon Tincture

Cinnamon

Cinnamon has such a distinctive, strong, sweet smell that it makes an excellent tincture on its own, and can be combined with other ointments for different smells.

Clove Tincture

Clove

Cloves too are strong enough and rich enough to be used alone.

Sage Tincture

Sage

This earthy, musky smell is just fine on its own.

Sleep Well Tincture

Lavender
Chamomile

This can be used in a sachet or a pillow to promote restful sleep and good dreams.

Nutmeg Tincture

Nutmeg

This tincture can be used alone, and can be smelled to wake up the senses, or can be used in money spells.

Peppermint Tincture

Peppermint

This mint-green tincture is used in money, purification and love rituals. Anoint sleep pillows. Try spearmint, too.

Wake Up Tincture

Cinnamon
Clove
Nutmeg
Pepper

This heady scent is perfect to wake up to.

Oily Skin Application

½ aloe gel

1 tbsp witch hazel

1 1/2 tsp cornstarch

3-4 drop peppermint essential oil

Mix the aloe, witch hazel, and cornstarch. Heat over a flame or even in the microwave, if you must, stirring every 20 seconds. When it turns into a clear gel-like substance, it is ready. Remove from heat. Keep stirring as it cools. The cornstarch will turn a clear aloe gel to an almost white cream color. Then add the peppermint. Store in an amber bottle. This can be applied to oily skin daily.

MOON RITUALS

One challenge that faces the urban wiccan is that of keeping track of the moon and her phases. Most cities, sadly, are victims of light pollution as well as water and air pollution. Finding the moon, let alone figuring out what stage it is in, is not often easy, especially when trying to peer through a haze of smog and fluorescence.

Spells and rituals often call for "moon baths", in which you, or a magickal object, is left to absorb the rays of the moon. In a city, this can be impossible to achieve on a regular basis. It is possible to travel to a less populated area, carrying spring water with you, and let the water sit in the rays of the moon. You can then keep the water in a container, preferably silver or crystal, for as long as you wish to use in your rituals when you get back to the city.

The following is a calendar of the phases of the moon.

List of the Moons

January – Storm Moon

February – Chaste Moon

March – Seed Moon

April – Hare Moon

May – Dyad (pair) Moon

June – Mead Moon

July – Wort (green plant) Moon

August – Barley Moon

September – Wine Moon

October – Snow Moon

November – Oak Moon

December – Wolf Moon

January ~ Storm Moon

This is the Moon the marks the last of the most severe storms of winter.

February ~ Chaste Moon

On this esbat, it may be a good idea to purify yourself, possibly abstaining from any earthly temptations during this month, if you wish, in order to greet the spring with a pure heart and soul.

March ~ Seed Moon

Sowing season and beginning of the new year.

April ~ Hare Moon

The rabbit, or hare, is often associated with Estora, and fertility.

May ~ Dyad Moon

The Latin word for "pair" refers to Castor and Pollux.

June ~ Mead Moon

This could refer to the fact that this was the time to collect hay from the meadows.

July ~ Wort Moon

This is a good time to dry and store wort plants.

August ~ Barley Moon

Persephone, Goddess of rebirth, carries barley at this time as a symbol of the harvest, and mentally prepares for the time in which she will descend back into the underworld, and fall and winter will begin.

September ~ Wine Moon

This moon marks the season of the grape harvest.

October ~ Snow Moon

In many parts of the world, October sees the first snowfall of the year.

November ~ Oak Moon

Oak was a sacred tree for the Romans

December ~ Wolf Moon

This nocturnal animal represents the "night"—or darkest part-- of the year.

The Blue Moon ~ Variable

A Blue Moon occurs when the moon with its 28 day cycle appears twice within the same calendar month.

The Black Moon ~ Variable

A Black Moon occurs when there are two dark cycles of the moon in any given calendar month.

Full Moon dates 2009

Year	Month	Day	Time	Day of week
2009	Jan	11	03:28	Sun
2009	Feb	9	14:51	Mon
2009	Mar	11	02:40	Wed
2009	Apr	9	14:58	Thu
2009	May	9	04:03	Sat
2009	Jun	7	18:13	Sun
2009	Jul	7	09:23	Tue
2009	Aug	6	00:57	Thu
2009	Sep	4	16:05	Fri
2009	Oct	4	06:11	Sun
2009	Nov	2	19:15	Mon
2009	Dec	2	07:33	Wed
2009	Dec	31	19:15	Thu

Full Moon dates 2010

Year	Month	Day	Time	Day of week
2010	Jan	30	06:19	Sat
2010	Feb	28	16:40	Sun
2010	Mar	30	02:28	Tue
2010	Apr	28	12:21	Wed
2010	May	27	23:09	Thu
2010	Jun	26	11:32	Sat
2010	Jul	26	01:38	Mon
2010	Aug	24	17:06	Tue
2010	Sep	23	09:19	Thu
2010	Oct	23	01:38	Sat
2010	Nov	21	17:28	Sun
2010	Dec	21	08:15	Tue

Full Moon dates 2011

Year	Month	Day	Time	Day of week
2011	Jan	19	21:23	Wed
2011	Feb	18	08:38	Fri
2011	Mar	19	18:12	Sat
2011	Apr	18	02:46	Mon
2011	May	17	11:10	Tue
2011	Jun	15	20:15	Wed
2011	Jul	15	06:41	Fri
2011	Aug	13	18:59	Sat
2011	Sep	12	09:28	Mon
2011	Oct	12	02:08	Wed
2011	Nov	10	20:18	Thu
2011	Dec	10	14:37	Sat

Full Moon dates 2011

Year	Month	Day	Time	Day of week
2012	Jan	9	07:31	Mon
2012	Feb	7	21:56	Tue
2012	Mar	8	09:42	Thu
2012	Apr	6	19:21	Fri
2012	May	6	03:37	Sun
2012	Jun	4	11:13	Mon
2012	Jul	3	18:54	Tue
2012	Aug	2	03:29	Thu
2012	Aug	31	14:00	Fri
2012	Sep	30	03:21	Sun
2012	Oct	29	19:52	Mon
2012	Nov	28	14:48	Wed
2012	Dec	28	10:22	Fri

CLEANSING YOURSELF OF THE CITY

Cleanses have become more and more popular as of late. When surrounded by the grime and energy of the common urban space, it's easy to feel as though a periodical detoxification is in order. Before embarking on a cleanse, remember to consult your health practitioner. Everyone is different, and not every program will work for you. As you conduct your cleanse, be vigilant about what your body is feeling. Make notes in a journal, if you wish. And remember to listen to your body's limits. If you feel sick or faint, call your wellness practitioner immediately.

The idea of cleansing is not all that new, and though Borroughs, the creator of the Master Cleanse, might currently be the most famous of the cleansers, the trend started with

Gerson Therapy. The therapy is based on dietary restriction, enzymes and detoxification, with some vitamin, mineral and biological supplementation. Dr. Max Gerson's belief was that toxic chemicals in the environment poison humans. He says denatured food grown on depleted soil, poisoned with pesticides, highly processed, and preserved with hundreds of dangerous chemicals causes disease.

Hyperalimentation, he asserted, was the best way to counter the negative effects of these omnipresent toxins.

This is accomplished through the consumption of 13 eight-ounce glasses of fresh, organic juices daily, supplemented by three large, organic, vegan meals, and numerous fruit and vegetable snacks throughout the day.

Gerson supplemented the hyperalimentation with a coffee enema that would stimulate the liver to produce bile, thereby flushing the undetectable toxins from the liver and making it ready to filter more from the bloodstream. He believed that chronic pain is most often the result of accumulated "toxicity" and that removing the toxins in this manner would provide instant pain relief of even the most persistent and acute pain.

Gerson prohibited nearly all animal products and all fats and oils except for flax-seed oil. All foods had to be fresh and organically grown, nothing could be processed, preserved, canned, bottled, boxed, frozen. The diet is salt-free, and avoids all supposed sources of "toxicity", including tobacco, alcohol, fluoride, pesticides, food chemicals and all pharmaceuticals.

Gerson, born in 1881, was very ahead of his time in recognizing the dangerous of processed foods and fertilized soil. Certainly, it can't hurt to eat healthfully and have a balanced diet.

You will see me put the word "toxins" in quotes, however, because none of the cleanses I'll talk about ever define what a toxin is. In reality, a toxin is an amount of something, not a property of something. For example, tomatoes, nutmeg, and even water can be poisonous if over ingested. I include all of this fasting stuff, however, because it seems very widespread in Wiccan, Shaman, and alternative medicine communities. I heard of the Master Cleanse, and it didn't work for me. This lead me to explore alternatives and I found some programs that seemed be reasonable, make sense, and helped me feel like I wasn't always saturated in the filth and grime that one finds in the air and on every surface, practically, in LA. Being clean on the inside makes you feel clean on the outside, I guess, which isn't easy when you're in a crowded environment, touching surfaces that hundreds of thousands of other people have touched, and breathing air that has been the repository for millions of tiny little particles of soot.

THE MASTER CLEASE

Also known as the Master Cleanser, the Lemonade Diet, and the Cleanse, this method of detoxification was created by Stanley Burroughs in 1941. Mr. Burroughs has been called a pioneer in the field of alternative medicine. He claims that the diet can purify body, mind, and spirit, ridding the dieter of toxins and impurities, and is a complete healing system.

Burroughs feels that the human body is constantly under assault from a variety of toxins and that the Cleanse is an ideal way to rid oneself of them. The cleanser must limit oneself to consuming only organic, natural laxative tea; water infused with sea salt; and a lemon mixture for at least ten days.

> **To make the lemon mixture:**
> Take the juice of 1/2 lemon (preferably organic)
> Mix with juice into 8 ounces of distilled water
> Add 1-2 Tbsp. of grade B maple syrup
> Add 1/8-1/4 tsp. cayenne pepper (red)

Burroughs instructs participants to consume as many 8-10 oz glasses as required according to body weight per day.

For example, if the participant weighs 100 pounds then she would drink half her weight in ounces.

Each ingredient of the lemon mixture performs a different function: Grade B maple syrup, according to Burroughs, contains a balance of positive and negative ions, and has a lower glycemic index than other sugars such as, say, honey or glucose. Diabetics are instructed to substitute blackstrap molasses for maple syrup using up to 1/4 tsp.

Lemons are included in order to cleanse mucous from the intestines, and the cayenne is said to act to dilate the blood vessels, thereby increasing circulation, and providing Vitamin A.

Before going to bed each night while on the fast, the participant is to drink a cup of natural laxative tea. In the morning, dieters should add two teaspoons of non-iodized sea-salt to a quart of lukewarm water, and drink the water as quickly as possible. An hour later, a trip to the toilet will be necessary and vast amounts of materials will be emptied from the digestive tract.

To end the fast, dieters are instructed to carefully add back orange juice, vegetable broth, and brown rice.

Many of my friends have done this fast with excellent results. I myself tried and ended up very sick within a period 72 hours, and had to cease and desist. Some swear by it; others claim that it's dangerous: in an interview with Web MD in an article published on Sept 11 2006, , physicians and dieticians claimed that the fast was not only useless, but dangerous. Readers were reminded that there has been no evidence offered that the cleanse augments the detoxification systems that the body already has in place.

Adherents claim that the effects of detoxification are long-lasting, but in his book about the cleanse, Mr. Burroughs provides no concrete definition of the word "toxins". Since the "toxins" cannot be observed or measured, there is no way to determine whether or not they have indeed been shed during the course of the cleanse. Additionally, no scientific information is provided to prove that the "toxins" are indeed harmful and require elimination. If indeed these toxins are harmful, can't one just abstain from ingesting them in the first place, instead of flushing them out? Why are they in all foods *except* for lemons, cayenne pepper, and maple syrup? And if the toxins are in food, then won't they return the minute the Cleanse is concluded and eating resumes?

Another important think to consider when evaluating the validity of the claims regarding "toxins" is that "toxic" is less a description of the property of a given substance than a description of its abundance. Water, for instance, can be toxic if too much at once is ingested. A young woman, in fact, recently died of water poisoning while in a contest hosted by a radio station to see who could drink the most water. Again, the diet does not seek to clarify exactly what it is about food that is "toxic" and in what amount.

JUICE FAST

Juice fasting is a type of fasting and detox diet in which the practitioner consumes only fruit and vegetable juices. These foods are digested rapidly as the juice digestion process expends only a small amount of energy. People choose to undergo juice fasts for various reasons and via various methods. Juice fasts are often marketed together with supplies, supplements and support groups.

They are generally undergone with the intent of detoxification for greater health, the theory being that less energy is expended on digestion of foods so more energy exists within the body to "expel toxins". As toxins are believed to lie within many of the human body's eliminative glands and organs, different juice fasts target different sections of the body. A large portion of juice fasters believe that abstaining from solid food allows the body to recover and heal itself from damage and fatigue caused by the unending stress of digestion.

Some loyal practitioners go so far as to partake in semi-annual week-long (or longer) periods of fasting in order to cyclically purify the body along with the nature's annual cycles. These semi-annual fasters and others may also partake in once-monthly, shorter (two or three days) periods of fasting. Some fasts involve a week-long trip to a spa resort, with Thailand being one especially popular destination.

Because pure juice contains little to no fiber, juice fasters often use an enema or an herbal or saltwater laxative during the time of fasting to efficiently expel waste from the intestines and colon.

The type of juice used in a juice fast can vary according to the specific goals of the participant. However, greens, cruciferous veggies, roots, fruit, and herbs are all possible ingredients for a juice fast.

I'm including it here because I've heard so many stories about friends who have done it, and loved it. I tried to do it once, and again ended up really sick. Because I'm hypoglycemic and very sensitive to spikes and ebbs in blood sugar, juice fasts are not for me. If you do this, make sure to consult with your health practitioner.

Hulda Clark's Kidney Cleanse
© 2004 by Hulda Regehr Clark, Ph.D., N.D.

* 1/2 cup dried hydrangea root, organic, (c/s)
* 1/2 cup gravel root, organic, (c/s)
* 1/2 cup marshmallow root, organic, (c/s)
* 4 bunches of fresh parsley
* ginger capsules
* Uva Ursi capsules
* Black Cherry Concentrate, 8 oz., tested
* vitamin B6, 250 mg
* magnesium oxide, 300 mg in powder form

Directions:

Measure 1/4 cup of each root and set them to soak, together, in 10 cups of water, using a stainless steel saucepan. After four hours or overnight, add 8 oz. black cherry concentrate, heat to boiling and simmer for 20 minutes.

Drink 1/4 cup as soon as it is cool enough. Pour the rest through a stainless steel strainer into a container and refrigerate it to consume later.

After thoroughly washing organic parsley, boil it in for five minutes, making sure that it's completely immersed in the water even when it comes to a rolling boil. Drink 1/4 cup of the water when it cools down enough. Freeze 1 pint and refrigerate the rest. Throw away the parsley.

Dose:

Each morning, pour together

3/4 cup of the root mixture
1/2 cup parsley water

Drink this mixture in divided doses throughout the day and keep it in the fridge between doses. Do not drink it all at once or you will get a stomach ache and feel pressure in your bladder. If your stomach is very sensitive, start on half this dose.

Save the roots after the first boiling, storing them in the freezer. After 13 days when your supply runs low, boil the same roots a second time, but add only 6 cups water and simmer only 10 minutes. This will last another 8 days, for a total of three weeks.

After three weeks, repeat with fresh herbs. You need to do the Kidney Cleanse for six weeks to get good results, longer for severe problems.

Also take:

* ginger capsules: 2 with each meal (6 a day)
* Uva Ursi capsules: 2 with each meal (6 a day)
* vitamin B6 (250 mg): one a day
* magnesium oxide (300 mg): one a day...

These supplements will aid in digestion, prevent flatulence, and give you extra energy.

ALTERNATIVES TO CLEANSES

One of the benefits of modern living is that we have a huge variety of resources to access. In LA, New York, Kansas City, Austin, Chicago, Seattle—really any major city—it's possible to find plenty of farmer's markets and health food stores that can help us to live healthy all the time, instead of using cleanses as quick fixes. This is my preference, although it's not always easy. Rather than rely on a week of sober eating and then returning to gobbling up all variety of starches and processed foods, I prefer to strive for a healthy lifestyle at all times. Here are some alternatives to cleanses, followed by healthy recipes for various Wiccan holidays.

AYURVEDA

How it came about

Ayurvedic medicine is a form of alternative medicine in use primarily in India. The word "Ayurveda", roughly translated, means "the science of long life". Ayurveda is claimed to deal with the measures of healthy living, along with therapeutic measures that relate to physical, mental, social and spiritual harmony and is also one among the few traditional systems of medicine involving surgery.

What does the diet consist of?

Diet is one of many elements involved in the holistic belief system of Ayurveda. Practitioners believe that food determines the effect on our body, and that effect can range from being one of emotion, to disease, to sickness. Adherents believe that food intake should maximize order and coherence in the body so as to maintain strength of the immune system. Moreover, consumption of this food take should be in partnership with a lifestyle that maximizes sound moral, spiritual, and emotional choices.

The breadth and depth of this whole, total life system is too detailed to be explored here with any depth. However, a sample of one of its aspects is provided herewith for examination and comparison to other diet and lifestyle systems included in this book.

Maharishi Ayurveda describes three kinds of toxins. The most common type is ama, which is a harmful by-product of digestion that builds up in the digestive tract when one's digestive process is either weak, overburdened, or trying to cope with the wrong foods.

If ama continues to build up, or is not flushed from the body, eventually it can seep through the digestive tract and spread. Once it settles in a specific area of the body, it can mix with and react to other tissues and wastes in the body, then becoming, amavisha. This is the second toxin, and is described as a more destructive, toxic type of ama.

The third type of toxin comes from outside the body and include pesticides, preservatives, additives, processed, and genetically engineered foods. Food that has rotted or gone bad and is filled with harmful bacteria also falls in this category. Other garavisha toxins include arsenic, lead, asbestos, chemicals in detergents and household supplies, poisons, air and water pollution, chemicals and synthetics in clothing, and recreational drugs.

While practitioners feel that amavisha and garavisha types of toxins should ideally be expressed by an ayurvedic health practitioner, the first kind of toxin can be cleansed of the body through diet and health practices.

One can identify a buildup of ama by a few telltale signs. For instance, general achiness, stiff joints, an unpleasant body odor, post-meal carb crashes, and a general lack of the ability to think clearly and function optimally can signal the presence of too much ama in the body. Not treating the ama can lead to diarrhea, or frequent colds and flu.

Adherents to this philosophy believe that it is best to avoid fried foods, hard cheeses, meats, leftovers, junk food, food empty in calories, processed foods, and rich desserts, as well as overly cold food and drinks. It is also important to eat the biggest meal at noon, to not skip meals, and to have consistent eating habits, as well as to have a regular daily routine. Stress reduction is also crucial to reducing the buildup of ama.

It is difficult to argue with a diet that calls for adherents to have consistent eating habits, minimize stress, and minimize exposure to, say arsenic. It is also difficult to find fault with a diet that calls for restricting consumption of fried, non-nutritive, overly processed, high sodium, high fat foods. It just takes a lot of conviction and discipline to constantly eat this mindfully.

MACROBIOTIC DIET

Some claim that the word "Macrobiotic" was found in the writings of Hippocrates. Others trace the macrobiotic methodology to Japanese philosophers and health practitioners', particularly one who is said to have cured himself of a serious illness by changing to a simple diet of brown rice, miso soup, and sea vegetables. The diet originally came to American consciousness by its direct translation, "the Unique Principal."

Followers of macrobiotics, like practitioners of Ayurveda, believe that food affects our lives more than is commonly thought, even having effects on emotional well being and happiness. Adherents select unprocessed, natural, foods, and instead of seeking meals from commercial, pre-prepared sources, espouse traditional methods of food preparation at home for family and friends.
Sources of food are ideally locally, organically grown. The diet can include whole grain cereals, beans, vegetables, fruit, seaweed and fermented soy products. All foods must, however, be combined in such a way as to balance yin and yang. Yin is said to be cold while yang is hot; yin is sweet,

yang is salty; yin is passive, yang is aggressive. Some strains of macrobiotic diets instead advocate dividing foods into the groups of principle and secondary pleasure. Others rephrase the balance of yin and yang to mean the balance of alkaline and acid. In any case, for most strains of the diet, balance is an important aspect.

Ohsawa, the Japanese educator that is rumored to have cured himself by subsisting on brown rice, miso, and veggies, described ten diets in total, with varying proportions of the following food groups: cereals, vegetables, soups, animal foods, salad and fruits, desserts, and beverages. The classic Macrobiotic diet consists of 50–60% whole grains, 30% vegetables, 5% soups like miso, and small portions of beans, nuts, seeds, seasonal fruit or fish.

In theory, unlike the raw foods, paleo, or blood type diet, the composition of macrobiotic dishes is also subject to the time of year the food has been produced, the time of day it is being consumed, and the ratio of oil to salt. In addition, the traditionally macrobiotic dish must use five colors and five flavors.

As in the raw foods diet, practitioners condone food preparation in various ways, including: steaming, boiling, raw, ohitashi, nishime, nitsuke, kinpira, sukiyaki, nabe, oven baking, baking in a pressure cooker, and, unlike the macrobiotic, paleo, ayurvedic, or raw foods diet, macrobiotic practitioners are allowed to prepare food tempura style, or fried.

Since macrobiotics originally came from Japan, it does not take a genius to observe that many aspects of macrobiotic cooking can be observed in traditional Japanese cuisine.

Like many alternative therapies, the macrobiotic diet not embraced by western medical science, with most of the controversy stemming from claims that the diet can cure cancer. Claims of this nature are purely anecdotal and not supported with clinical trials or medical research. Perhaps as a result, the American Medical Association opposes the macrobiotic diet.

Critics also point out that the macrobiotic includes a very limited source of fruits and vegetables and, in its most rigid and strict variances, can also be lacking in protein, calcium, vitamin B12, folate, and iron. Overly rapid weight loss can also result if participants do not ease into the diet, particularly persons who are used to a diet high in fat. In its original form, the macrobiotic diet required foods to be slowly eliminated from the diet until only rice and beans were consumed.

A macrobiotic diet can also be inappropriate for children, cancer patients, gluten-sensitive enteropathy , pregnant women, or people with or cereal grain allergies.

Proponents of the diet, however, point to the lack of obesity in Japan as evidence for its healthful nature, as well to a significant amount of personal testimonials.

Raw foods gained some notoriety in the 1900's, as a small group of vocal proponents claimed that a diet of raw fruits and vegetables is the ideal diet for humans.

More recently, In 1975, computer programmer-turned-nutritionist Viktoras Kulvinskas published *Survival Into the 21st Century*. This book was followed by Leslie Kenton's book *The New Raw Energy* in 1984. Currently, several books are available on the market that provide easy recipes, lifestyle guides, and attempts to supplement these claims with scientific data.

A raw food diet consists eating only uncooked and unprocessed, and often organic foods. In order for a food to qualify as "uncooked", it can only be heated or kept up to a certain temperature. This temperature varies among the different forms of the diet, and ranges from 92°F to 118°F. Some practitioners of this lifestyle believe that for optimum health, at least 75% of consumed food must be raw. Freezing food is generally considered acceptable amongst raw foodists.

Raw food diets include raw fruits, raw vegetables, raw nuts, raw seeds, and may include raw unpasteurized dairy products, raw meat, raw eggs, and raw honey. Raw foods advocates romanticize early man, and feel that the diet of the Stone Age man is more ideal than that of Modern Man. Raw foodists feel that heating or overcooking food degrades or destroys these enzymes, putting a burden on the body's own enzyme production, leading to toxicity in the body, and eventually to obesity and to chronic disease.

Proponents also claim that raw foods contain bacteria and other micro-organisms that stimulate the immune system and assist the digestive system by populating the digestive tract with beneficial bacterial blooms.
The benefits of the diet are said to include: a stable body mass index, clear skin, more energy, and chronic and long lasting superior health.

Raw food contains little or no saturated fat and trans fats. It is also low in sodium, high in potassium, magnesium, folate, fiber, and phytochemicals. According to Cathy Wong's article on altmedicine.com, a study published in the Journal of Nutrition found that consumption of a raw food diet contributed to low cholesterol and triglycerides.

Another obvious benefit is that the diet eschews the consumption of processed junk foods, foods of dubious quality, and foods high in sodium and refined sugars.

Raw food diets have, however, sustained criticism for being restrictive and time consuming, and caution that the diet needs to be undertaken with great care so as to consume appropriate levels of vitamins and nutrients.

Critics also point out that whether or not foods are raw or cooked, the proteins and other macronutrients contained within are broken down into base amino acids during the digestion process.

While advocates also assert that it is impossible to determine the amount of time, or even the feasibility of adjusting to a diet of cooked food since cooking food is uniquely a human experience. Critics, however, counter that this ignores the large amount of evidence which clearly shows the change in human teeth and jaw structure, and the correlation of these changes to the controlled use of fire.

Advocates also argue that since animals do not cook their food and they don't get degenerative diseases, if humans didn't cook their food, humans wouldn't get these diseases either. This, however, is untrue, as animals in the wild do get cancer and other degenerative brain diseases.

And of course, critics warn that cooking dairy and meat products kill harmful bacteria, and that the consumption of raw eggs and dairy increases the risk of consuming salmonella, and various parasites.

Healthy Recipes

Good Morning Cornmeal Mush

1 cup cornmeal

1 cup cold water

1 tsp. salt

1 tsp. sugar

2 3/4 cups water in a pan

Bring the 2 3/4 cups of water to a boil. In bowl, combine the cornmeal, 1 cup water, salt, and sugar. Gradually add this mixture to the boiling water, stirring constantly. Cover and cook over low heat for 10-15 minutes. Pour into a shallow loaf pan. Chill in refrigerator overnight. In the morning, turn it out of the pan onto a platter or flat countertop. Cut into 1/2 inch slices. Toast in a toaster oven at 325 degrees until golden brown. Serve with cinnamon, butter buds, or light margarine, and enjoy!

Makes 6 servings.

Sun God Turkey Sausage and Eggs

1 lb. Turkey Sausage, or Veggie Sausage

4 hard boiled egg whites

1/4 cup butter/margarine

1/4 cup all purpose flour

2 cups milk

1- 16oz bag frozen fresh corn

1 cup soft whole grain bread crumbs

1 cup coarsely ground turnip

1 zucchini squash sliced

1/2 tsp. salt

In a frying pan, cook sausage and turnip, drain. In a sauce pan boil zucchini slices until tender, drain. Slice two of the eggs and line the bottom of a 1 1/2 qt casserole dish. For second layer, top eggs with 1/2 of the zucchini slices, put other half aside. In the sauce pan melt butter/margarine; blend in flour, salt, and a dash of pepper. Add milk all at once. Cook, stirring constantly, until mixture thickens and bubbles. Stir in sausage mixture and corn. Pour 1/2 mixture over eggs, arrange the rest of the zucchini slices, pour in rest of mixture. Slice the remaining two eggs and arrange on top of mixture. Sprinkle with bread crumbs and bake at 375 degrees for 30 minutes or until heated all the way through.   Makes 6 servings.

Stuffed Mushrooms

2- 6oz cans of broiled mushroom crowns

1 tbs. finely chopped onion

1 tsp. vegetable oil

1/4 cup smoked cheese spread or vegan soy cheese

1 tbs. catsup

1/4 cup finely chopped turnip*

1 tsp. minced garlic

Fine soft while grain bread crumbs

Drain the cans of broiled mushroom crowns. Hollow out and chop up enough of the pieces to make 3 tbs. In a sauce pan, combine the mushroom pieces, onion, turnip, and garlic. Add the vegetable oil and cook slowly over a low heat. Stir in the cheese spread and catsup. Stuff the slightly cooled mixture into the mushroom crowns and place on a greased cookie sheet. Sprinkle tops with the fine soft bread crumbs. Bake at 425 degrees for 6-8minutes.

Oven Hash

1 cup coarsely ground beef

OR

1 cup textured vegetable protein

OR

1 cup ground turkey

1 cup coarsely ground potatoes

1/4 cup coarsely ground onion

1/4 cup snipped fresh parsley

2 tsp. Worcestershire sauce

1- 6oz can evaporated milk

1/4 cup fine dry whole grain bread crumbs

1 tbs. butter/margarine/light margarine melted

In frying pan, combine and cook beef, potatoes, onion, parsley, and Worcestershire sauce, and evaporated milk. Remove from heat and turn out into a 1 qt casserole dish. Mix bread crumbs with melted butter/margarine and sprinkle on top. Bake in oven at 350 degrees for 30 minutes.

Makes 4 servings.

Beltane Marigold Custard

2 cups nonfat milk soy milk

1 cup unsprayed marigold petals

1/4 tsp. salt

3 tbsp. sugar

1 to 2-inch piece vanilla bean or 1 tsp vanilla extract

3 egg yolks, slightly beaten

1/8 tsp. allspice

1/8 tsp. nutmeg

1/2 tsp. rose water

Using a clean mortar and pestle reserved for cooking purposes, pound marigold petals. Or, crush with a spoon. Mix the salt, sugar and spices together. Scald milk with the marigolds and the vanilla bean. Remove the vanilla bean and add the slightly beaten yolks and dry ingredients. Cook on low heat. When the mixture coats a spoon, add rose water and cool.

Top with whipped cream, garnish with fresh marigold petals

Index

Y

www.ingramcontent.com/pod-product-compliance
Lightning Source LLC
Chambersburg PA
CBHW051722090426
42738CB00010B/2039